CONFESSIONS OF A CHURCH BOY

D'MAINE ROMARR FREELAND

Freeland Family Enterprise

Copyright © 2020 by D. Romarr Freeland

All rights reserved. This book or any portion thereof may not be reproduced or used in any manner whatsoever without the express written permission of the publisher except for the use of brief quotations in a book review.

Printed in the United States of America

First Printing, 2020

ISBN 978-0-578-80813-0

Freeland Family Enterprise

32 Artist Lake Blvd, Ste 2

Middle Island, NY 11953

www.freelandfamilyenterprise.org

CONTENTS

Acknowledgments   vii
Foreword   ix

Chapter 1   1
Chapter 2   11
Chapter 3   17
Chapter 4   19
Chapter 5   24
Chapter 6   26

In the memory of Nana Helen Bostic
In honor of Pop Bishop Alvin Freeland
To the Legacy of Naomi Skai Freeland and Colbi Justin Civil

ACKNOWLEDGMENTS

I would like to take this opportunity to appreciate the best and most important part of me, and that is my lovely wife, Shamel Freeland. "A wise woman builds her home, but a foolish woman tears it down with her own hands." Thank you for lending your wisdom to make sure our house is a home. Your dedication is invaluable. I love you, babe. You are the lifeline to our Freeland clan.

I would also like to acknowledge the GPS that led me to greatness, Bishop Archie L McInnis. You have imparted so much wisdom in me regarding ministry, family, and business. I am forever indebted to you for trusting me as your son in the Gospel.

Last but not least, to the person who pushed and helped me to make this dream a reality, Wanza Leftwich, my prayer for you is that GOD grants you your heart's desire. You are my ambassador and the reason for me being able to leave a legacy for my children and my children's children.

My prayer is that this book forces change in whoever reads it. Confession is not always easy, but it's possible. With Christ, we can do anything but fail.

FOREWORD

Jesus said unto Peter, "... upon this rock I will build my church; and the gates of hell shall not prevail against it."

— MATTHEW 16:18

One of the wonderful things about the church is that it is blessed by Jesus Christ himself. The church is the body of Christ, a living, breathing organism. The church is a body of believers whose head and chief leader is Jesus Christ. The history of the church has proven that even with much persecution and bloodshed, it steadily grows. The church has been a beacon light for people of all nations for thousands of years. Because of the church, countless lives have been changed through the power of Jesus Christ. Many of those have become great leaders and world-changers in our society today. There are many testimonies worldwide of how God and His church

FOREWORD

has changed the lives of even the worst of the worst and made them extraordinary men and women of God.

One of the most powerful things that I love about the church is that the gates of hell shall not prevail against it. Gates are used as barriers to prevent entrance without permission. The gates of hell are designed to prevent forward movement or progress. People are blocked every day without any knowledge of it. The gates of hell keep them blocked. There is no forward movement. They are stuck and produce no change. Everything remains the same. However, believers who belong to the church of Christ are unstoppable. The gates of hell shall not prevail against them. Because of Christ, the church is unstoppable, and you are unstoppable if you belong to the church of Christ.

This book, written by D'Maine Freeland, will reveal the awesomeness of our God. It shows how, in one moment, you could be headed for disaster with no hope. But after one encounter with God and His Church, your disaster can turn into a divine interception of grace. D'Maine Freeland is an example that the church is not just a religious institution but rather a life alternative that gives hope to the hopeless and unlimited possibilities. The way the Lord has blessed D'Maine Freeland, his career, and his family will cause anyone that doubts the church and the power of God to think again after reading this miraculous story of *Confessions of a Church Boy*.

Bishop Archie L. McInnis II
Full Effect Gospel Ministries & Full Effect Churches
General Overseer

CONFESSIONS OF A CHURCH BOY

CHAPTER 1

I can remember like it was yesterday. I was seven years old, and my mom had just left my biological father. She got an apartment in Marcus Garvey Village, so we left my grandmother's house and moved into our new complex. It was a two-bedroom apartment.

The following Sunday, my mom took us to a church that was right across the street from where we lived. The church was named First Baptist Church of Brownsville. When we entered this church, my life really began to take a new course. At that time, I was too young to realize that this is where we would begin our new life.

My mother made new friends, and with new friends came a new lifestyle. My grandmother had become very sick, and I had no knowledge of it because I was too young to understand. As time went on, things seemed to be going well. I did not know that my mother was selling narcotics for my uncle. I can remember all the parties that used to be held at our house every Friday and Saturday. I could count on the house being full of people laughing, joking, and watching VHS movies.

My sister and I were confined to our bedrooms. Sometimes we put our ears to the door to listen. We wanted to know what my mother and her friends were laughing and joking about. We would fake occasional trips to the bathroom to try to see what was happening, but my mother was exceptionally good at shielding us from the truth – the real lifestyle she was involved in.

I thought we had a good life because everyone seemed to love hanging out with my mother. At church, everyone would laugh and talk about the good time they had at our house over the weekend. *My mom really knows how to make people happy.* I did not have a clue about what was really going on. My mother made everything look so easy. Every weekend when she would come home from work, she always had two or three new VHS tapes. She rented them from a video store that was connected to her job in the city when she worked for the union. My mother was only 28 years old.

When my friends came over to my house, they were so amazed to see the floor model TV and two VHS recorders we had in our apartment. I did not know how much status came with having those things because my mother always kept us in the dark about how much they really cost.

On Sundays, we would go to church and meet new people. I somehow someway grew a deep affection for being in church. It was the place that I seemed to have the most fun. When others used to say they couldn't wait until Saturday to watch cartoons, I found myself not being able to wait until Saturday to go to choir rehearsal with my mom. At first, I used to play around in the church when she first brought me. As I got a little older, I wanted to join the kids' choir, known as The Sunbeam Choir. We sang every second Sunday of the month.

Every Saturday, I found myself wanting to run to the church and be in the church and stay for all the rehearsals. I was sad when rehearsals were over. I clearly remember going to one rehearsal, and I heard this voice singing while I was in the back of the church. My friends and I were playing, but this voice caught my attention at nine years old. I did not know what it was about that voice that kept getting my attention. All I wanted to know was who the person was behind that voice.

The voice belonged to Alvin Freeland. At the time, he was just plain old Professor Freeland. Every time he sang, I would be amazed at how it sounded. When he opened his mouth, not only did he sing well, but he dressed very well. Every time I saw him, he always had on the best of everything. I used to ask my mom, "Who is that guy? He sings good." Then I was extra amazed because he played the piano and sang at the same time.

My mother told me he was the minister of music of the church. Professor Freeland became another reason for me to love going to the church on Saturdays and Sundays. I was always so excited when Saturday and Sunday came because I knew I would see the man who dressed nice and sang so great. I loved being around the church. I used to do everything in my power just to get there. I was in love with the preaching, and I enjoyed the singing. I enjoyed the laughter and all of the praises of worship that went up every time these people came together in one building.

I was so in love with the church that I never paid attention to the fact that my mother stopped going as often as she used to after a while. I would find myself getting dressed early on Sunday morning just to go across the street because I couldn't wait for the church to open. I couldn't wait to be in there and see all of my friends and be around people that made me feel good. Of course, I could not wait to see Professor Freeland.

One day he saw me following him around, and he asked me, "What do you want, kid? Why you keep following me?"

"I don't know."

"Well, if you're going to keep following me, then hold my bag."

That was the best moment that ever happened to me. I was the proud bag holder of Professor Freeland. As time went on, I began to get more attached to the church and to everything that was happening in and around the church. I wanted to be a part of everything. I wanted to sing in the choir, play the drums, and work the sound system. Whatever needed to be done in the church, I wanted to do it.

I had gotten myself so involved in the church that I never paid attention to what had begun to happen at home. As I was falling in love with the church, things had begun to go crazy at home with my mom. My grandmother had gotten ill and passed away. I remember being in the waiting room with my sister at Kings County Hospital. We were too young to go into the room. I heard my mother let out a big scream. Shortly afterward, she came to the waiting room and hugged me and my sister. She sat on the cold rubber hospital chair and said, "Grandma is gone, okay? She went to heaven."

She started crying even harder and gasped for air. I do not know what my sister did, but I cried too. I knew I wasn't crying because my grandma was gone because I have heard so much about this place called heaven by Rev. Lyons at church. I thought grandma was in a good place, but to see my mother crying and gasping for air this way scared me. I got this nauseating feeling in my stomach seeing her like that.

Later that night, as we were going home, my mother told my uncle, "I'm gonna need some for tonight."

I did not know what she was talking about, but I knew it was something cause when we got home, she went swiftly to her room and closed the white door with the wood letters DEE on it.

Little did I know that was the beginning of the end. From that moment, the most I saw of my mother was when she closed the white door with the DEE on it. But I never stopped going to church.

By then, I was nine years old, and Professor Freeland was now POP. He and my mother had a conversation about him being my godfather because I spent so much time with him. The church had become my second home. Every time the doors were open, I was there doing something. It did not matter what day of the week nor what time it was. If the doors were open, I was there. But when the doors were closed and locked, I was on the streets.

At this point, my mother was totally consumed by crack cocaine. She only came out to get her fix and then went back home and stayed in the house. She would not go anywhere. All the people from the weekend parties disappeared, and it was just me and my sister. My next-door neighbor took a liking to my sister and would take care of her, feed her, and buy her clothes and things of that nature. She didn't bother with me because she already had two boys of her own.

So I had to make do the best way I could. I started

stealing from the neighborhood grocery stores just to eat. Some nights I would go to a friend's house and try to stay as long as I could so that I could have a chance to eat with them when it was time for dinner. As time went on and I got older, I began to get close to other church members and began to hang out with Damien, who lived in the same Marcus Garvey projects with me. His mom worked for a bank, so that worked out great. I would hang with Damien and stay at his house until his mom came home at 11:30 p.m.

There was nothing for me at home except a closed white door with DEE on it. Whenever I knocked on the door, she would say, "Don't come in here; just go to your room." That was the routine.

※

I was now in my first year of Junior High School. Every weekday I woke up and got my sister up and ready to go to school. My sister went to a different school then. She needed more help in school. There was a lady at the church who was also a teacher at a school not too far from where we lived, so my sister went there with her.

After a while, POP figured out what was going on with my mother and would give me $5 every Sunday and say, "This is for you for the week."

It doesn't sound like much now, but back then, I was rich. Besides, he would always give me more when I saw him during the week.

Then came the summer of my 12th birthday. Early in the morning, there was a knock on the door. I answered because my mom stopped answering the door for anyone. The neighborhood custodian looked at me and said,

"Where is your mother? You guys have to leave."

I didn't know what was going on. I went to wake my mother up, but before I could get her, the marshals had already come in and started throwing our stuff into boxes. I started to panic. I didn't know what to do, so I grabbed some change and ran to the closest pay phone and called POP.

When he answered, I was talking so fast and crying that he told me to slow down and explain to him what was going on. By the time I caught my breath enough to tell him, the time had run out. I had to put another coin in the payphone to call him back. After speaking to him, he told me to calm down, go back with my mother and sister, and have my mom call him. When I returned, my mother said, "Pack some clothes. We have to leave. We are being evicted."

I did not fully understand what that meant. I was only able to grab three pairs of pants and a few shirts. Later that night, we had to go to Downtown Brooklyn and wait in this building that had this nasty disinfecting smell that made me sick to my stomach. And it was there we waited until they found a shelter with enough room to place us. There we were in some building on hard plastic seats in the middle of the night, and all I could think was, *how am I going to get to church now?*

Am I ever going to see POP again?

Will we ever be able to go back home?

What about our things?

So many thoughts were running through my head. I had totally forgotten that it was my birthday.

Eventually, they called us and gave my mother a paper for us to go to a new shelter on Catherine Street in Manhattan by the

Brooklyn Bridge. I thought to myself, *this is good. We can still go to church. Just take the 3 train straight there.*

Living in a shelter, you had a curfew, and if you were not in by that time, you could not come back in until the next day. If your bed was given to someone, you had to redo the process all over again. Our curfew hours were 7 a.m.-11 p.m. Sun-Thurs, and 7 a.m.-12 a.m. Fri-Sat. It took about two weeks for us to get used to the new way of living. We had to get up early to use the public showers. That was scary for me because I had to wash in a public shower with about 6 to 10 other men I did not know.

My mother and sister went to the bathroom together. I was a boy, so I had to go to the bathroom alone. My mother stood at the door of the men's restroom and waited for me to come out. Then we had to stand in a long line for breakfast. We had to move fast because breakfast was only from 7 to 9 a.m. If you were too far back in line, they would cut it off and say you would have to wait until lunch at 11 a.m., but by that time, we would be gone.

My mother took us to Brooklyn every day so that we would not have to stay in the shelter. We didn't have any money for the train. She would tell us to go under the turnstile, and she would do the same. When we got to Brooklyn, she let me hang with my friends in Brownsville, and she and my sister would go somewhere else.

She always reminded me, "Make sure you meet us at the 3 train at 9 p.m. so we can go back to the shelter. We can't miss curfew." We did this for the remaining of the summer

The summer went by fast, and it was time for school again. School was very hard for me because I saw the kids looking nice and having loose-leaf notebooks and JanSport book bags. I had the black and white composition book and plain book bag they gave to all kids at the shelter. I guess that's the reason I don't buy black and white composition books to this day.

I can remember just sitting in class and looking at everyone and wishing I could be them. They all looked so happy and knew where they were going and what they were going to do when they got home. That was a luxury I didn't have but wanted so badly. The only thing I knew was that I had to make sure I got to the Rockaway Ave station by 9 p.m. so we could keep our beds in the shelter.

As time went on, I begged my mother every Sunday to let me go to church.

"No, because I'm not going, and no one would be there to bring you home."

Why did she say that? I immediately called POP and told him what she said, and he said, "Put her on the phone." Next thing I know, on Sunday, I was back at church, and it felt so refreshing. I was able to see everyone.

At church, the people smiled, hugged me, and told me how much they missed seeing me. Some of the mothers of the church even gave me money. Man! I was so happy to be there and to hear Rev. Lyons preach and my POP sing.

I was in heaven.

I enjoyed myself so much that I used to get mad when I heard people say, "These services are too long. I want to go home."

In my mind, church was my home because it was the only place I felt safe.

The time would come when I had to leave. I would get in the car with POP and get really quiet and depressed. I knew that at the end of the ride back to the shelter, I would have to wait six more days to come back to church.

POP knew what I was feeling. He always gave me $10 and a hug, and then he'd say, "I love you, Nanu." He called me by the nickname he had given me. I knew there was nothing he could do because I had to be with my mother. Each time I got out of the car, I took a deep breath and went through those big red doors and the metal detectors to the shelter.

CHAPTER 2

Just as I started getting used to the routine of things, life took another turn. It was a Sunday night, and POP dropped me off at the shelter. As usual, he gave me money, and I headed to my room. When I got to the room, my mother nor my sister was there. I decided to go looking for them in other rooms. By this time, we had made a few friends in the shelter and with some of the guards. I had to be careful looking for them because if the guards or counselors heard that I was looking for my mom, they would take me downstairs to the office and call BCW (Bureau of Child Welfare). So, as I quietly looked for them, I learned that no one saw or heard from them all day. It was past curfew, so I went to the room, turned out the lights, and prayed they would come in sometime before bed check.

The first bed check was at 12:30 a.m. The next bed check was at 3:30a m. When 12:30 a.m. came, my mom and sister were not there. I acted like I was asleep, but I heard the counselor say to the security guard, "If she's not here by the second bed check, we will take him down to BCW and let them deal with him."

Well, that was all I needed to hear. When the counselor and security guard left my room, I snuck to the payphone at the end of the hall. I immediately called POP and told him what they said.

"Can you get out? Are you able to get to the train? You can come here."

"Yes!" I replied.

That was all I needed to hear. I went back to the room, got dressed, and snuck out the back door. I can still hear the alarm ringing. I ran so fast to the A train to go to Bedford-Stuyvesant, where Pop lived.

Once I arrived at Pop's house, I was extremely tired and scared at the same time. Although I knew I was safe, I still wondered what happened to my mother and my sister. *Were they okay? Were they dead? Were they alive and looking for me?*

All these questions were swimming around in my head until I eventually went to sleep. The next morning POP woke me up for school. I smelled bacon and eggs cooking. I thought to myself, *somebody is eating good this morning*. I was so used to the processed shelter food. When I came out of the room, there she was -- my Nana (Pop's mother). I never really met her before because she worked nights.

Every time I came over, she was not there, but I heard so much about her. When I came out of the room, it was like Christmas.

"Go to the bathroom and wash your face," she said.

I stood there for a minute in complete shock. It hit me that the good smelling eggs and bacon was for me.

"Did you hear me? Go wash your face and hands so you can eat."

While washing my hands and face, I could hear Pop and Nana talking, but I did not quite understand what they were saying. As I came out of the bathroom, their conversation stopped. I sat down and ate while Nana ironed some of Pop's clothes he put out for me.

Man, that was the best food I ever had. The eggs had cheese melted on them, the bacon was perfect, and the toast was nicely brown with just the right amount of butter and jelly on it. It was the first time I ever had wheat bread, which I called brown bread. When I finished eating, Nana told me to take a bath.

"Go take a bath so you can get dressed," she said.

I became very confused.

I was not familiar with this routine. I went into the bathroom and came out so fast that Nana and Pop looked at me.

"There's no way you took a bath that quick. Nonetheless, it's getting late, so let's go."

Pop dropped me off at school. He told me how to get back to his house by bus once school was over. I was full of so many different emotions. I just had the best meal I had ever eaten, a good night's sleep, and nice fresh clothes on, but I still had not heard from my mother or sister. That day in school was a total loss for me. I was not able to concentrate on anything. I wanted to know where my mom and sister were.

An entire week passed, and I had not heard from my mom. Living with Pop and Nana, I met Aunt Betty and my two cousins, Sabrina and Sonja. They lived downstairs. Things seemed to be coming together well.

On Sunday we went to church and had a great time. Just as I

was starting to feel better about things, Pop came into my room and dropped some heartbreaking news on me.

"Get your things. Your mother is here, and you have to go."

"Why do I have to go? I can't stay here with you?" I was confused.

I did not want to leave. Life was getting better for me. Nana made breakfast every morning, Pop gave me $5 for school, and when I got home, I did my homework then went downstairs to hang out with my cousins.

"Why do I have to leave?"

"You can't stay here if your mother wants you. She has custody of you."

Reluctantly, I got my things together. I cried. I could not believe I had to leave. I went downstairs and there she was. Part of me was happy to see her, and the other part of me was sad because I had to leave a place that made me happy. I went outside and got into her new boyfriend's car. My sister was in the back seat. I gave her a big hug. I missed her so much, and I believed she missed me too because she hugged me just as hard.

While sitting in the car, I saw Pop talking to my mom, but I could not hear what they were saying.

"Are you okay, Charlene?" I asked my sister.

"Yes," she replied.

"Where did y'all go?"

"We went to mommy's friend's house."

"Are you going to school?" I asked her.

"Yes. Mommy and her boyfriend take me to school and pick me up."

When my mom got back in the car, I had to ask her why I couldn't stay with Pop.

"We have nowhere to go, and you have to be with me so we can get back into the shelter."

So it was back to the welfare office that night and to the shelter again. We must have sat in that welfare office at least until one in the morning. My former routine of life returned. The only difference this time is that instead of traveling on the train, we would be in her boyfriend's car. He couldn't stay in the shelter with us, but he would meet up with my mother and take us back to the shelter just about every night.

While in the shelter, I would pray nightly.

"Lord, please help us get out of this place. Lord, please help me get back to church." I was too young to understand what I was doing, but I learned from going to church and Sunday School that if I just talked to God, He would hear me.

Some time passed, and I believe my mom grew tired of all the stipulations that came along with being at the shelter. One Friday, we went to my Aunt Boobie's place in the Brownsville projects. I was happy about going there because that meant I could go to church. I expected to stay for the weekend, but we never left. I guess my aunt and mother came up with an agreement that allowed us to stay there. Aunt Bobbie had a three-bedroom apartment, and she allowed my mother to have one room. I was too young to know if there was some kind of financial agreement between them. All I know is that I was walking distance from the church and my old neighborhood.

I was free to do whatever I wanted to do. My mom would take my sister and leave. I did not mind because I was able to go back to my routine of going to the church every time it was open. It was even better now. On the weekends, I started to stay at Mother Burgess' house. Let me tell you something. Staying at her house was so much fun. Their family unit was amazing and breathtaking. I became close with her son, Charles, and her daughter, Bernadette. We all went to church together.

I was able to stay with Mother Burgess from Friday to Sunday. I realized again that the church created a safe haven for me. Philippians 4:19 (KJV) is so true. "But my God shall supply all your needs according to his riches in glory by Christ Jesus." The church supplied me with a new family and made sure I experienced the family bonding and love that I did not know was so important and essential to life.

Before I knew it, I had a new routine. I went to my aunt's house for the week, and I spent the weekends with the Burgess family, who lived around the corner from the church. This was how I spent my junior high school years.

CHAPTER 3

During the summer of 1990, I went from staying at Mother Burgess' house on the weekend to actually living there. I later found out that Pop arranged for me to stay there. He gave her money every week for me to stay there. I did not understand everything, but I knew I was able to stay somewhere that had a family structure. I was happy, and that is what mattered.

By this time, my mom and sister had totally disappeared from my life, but God filled the void with Pop and Mother Burgess. I did not have my natural parents, but I had them. The holidays were full of fun and laughs. However, I still felt empty because I knew I would not see anyone who was blood-related. I was unofficially adopted into the family.

I used to wonder why my blood family didn't want me or was not concerned enough about me to know where I was. I would mask the feelings by emerging myself into Super Mario Brothers on Nintendo, and before long, the lonely feeling would disappear. Most of my childhood is really a blur, but all memories I do have are that of Sundays at First Baptist Church of Brownsville. Most kids have memories of family events and outings, but my memories are full of church services and gospel concerts I attended with Pop. Pop sang, or he would go to support his friends that were singers. The more I think about it, the more I realize that from about the age of 9 to 15 years of age, everything I did was centered around God. Although there are many blank spots in my childhood memory, I mostly remember the ones that included some sort of church function and the feeling of me not fitting in at school. I acted totally different from the kids my age.

There were times I would try to do things to fit in with the kids at school, but it never felt right. I would always hear Pop in my head, telling me, "The only peer pressure you have is me." That kept me from going too far. Furthermore, I always felt that if I did anything too crazy, God would take away the people that were raising me. Truth be told, everything they did for me, God made it possible. I felt that if I did anything crazy, God would change their hearts and minds, and I would not have anyone.

CHAPTER 4

In January 1991, I started hanging out with my friends from the block. I began to feel like a man since the bond we were forming felt a lot like the bond I had with my friends at church. But there was a difference; instead of constant joy and laugher, we were scared and afraid we were going to get hurt or end up in jail. I always knew that the things we did were not right, but I did it anyway.

I felt like these guys would protect me and help me if we ever got caught. And then it happened. I was riding on the train with about 9 or 10 other guys. We were talking about what we were going to do when we got to the city. Long story short, by the end of the day, I had a $400 ski coat.

I was both scared and amazed at what happened because it was so quick. When I got home later that day, Mom Burgess asked, "Where did you get such an expensive coat?"

I don't quite remember what my answer was, but I thought I

got away with it. That is until about two days later when I came home from school wearing the jacket and Pop was on the steps waiting for me.

I was shocked to see him because it was totally unlike him to be there, especially so early in the week. He made me sit down and began to ask questions about the jacket. I could not come up with any story that made sense. After about 20 minutes of him poking holes in all the stories I tried to give him, he finally asked, "Where did you steal this coat from?"

"I went to the city with a bunch of my friends," I stuttered.

I could not hold it in any longer. He didn't even beat me, but the lecture I got after admitting what I did was so severe I think it hit deeper than any physical beating I could ever get. By the end of the conversation, I was grounded until Christmas break, and I had to meet him at the church every day after school to help clean the church. There was no negotiating that, and the stolen coat was the only coat I was allowed to wear for the rest of the entire winter.

Now that I look back on it, I know it was nothing but God who intervened on my behalf because who knows what that one situation would have evolved into. No matter what I did or where I went, I always ended up back at church.

As the summer approached, I was ready to rejoin all my friends and resume whatever shenanigans awaited, but as always, GOD interrupted me.

That summer, I moved to Bedford Stuyvesant to help Pop take care of Nana. At first, I was upset because I wanted to hang out, but I came around. Although Nana was sick, she showered me with so much love and attention that the world seemed to disappear, leaving only me and her.

She would say to me, "Butter (my nickname), let's eat some

Chinese food today." She always wanted shrimp and broccoli with boneless chicken.

"Get what you want, but you better eat it all." She would hand me $20, and off I went.

I think I would run all the way there and back so that I could hear her sang when I got back.

"Children, go where I send thee. How will I send thee? I'm gonna send thee one by one, born, born, born in Bethlehem."

Then we would say grace, eat and laugh at whatever was on television. By the end of the summer, those days began to disappear as the cancer began to really take a toll on Nana. She became very weak and would sleep more and more, but I didn't care. I stayed right there in her room, sitting on the floor at the foot of her bed watching television. I was ready to get whatever she needed. Sometimes I would fall asleep, and Pop would make me go to bed. I didn't want to move just in case Nana needed me.

As I look back now, I realize why I was so attached. She filled that void that was left by my mother, leaving me in the shelter alone. I felt if I stayed right where Nana needed me, she wouldn't leave me. As time went on, Nana grew weaker and weaker, and the trips to the hospital were more frequent. Still, somewhere in the back of my mind, I thought that things would get better and go back to the way they were, but that never happened.

I still remember that last trip to Sloan Kettering hospital. Nana was in so much pain they had to put her in a medically induced coma. I didn't understand what was happening. I just remember Pop laying over her hospital bed, kissing her, and saying, "It's alright, mother. You can go now. We'll be okay."

I spent the entire ride back home trying to figure out what

was going on. Once we got home, Pop went to his room, and Aunt Betty, Sabrina, Sonja, and I were all in the living room, still in a state of what I would now call shock. Pop came from his room and said, "The doctor just called, and mother is gone!"

I can still remember that night like it just happened. My aunt burst into tears. My cousins were sitting on the couch, and I stood between the kitchen and living room. I was numb to everything around me. I was lost for words with no feelings. Everything just faded to black. Needless to say, the next few days were a total blur. I don't remember much going forward until the day of the funeral.

The funeral was amazing. I know it may sound crazy to say, but that's the only word that comes to mind because it was the first time I had ever seen anyone wear white to a funeral. The church was filled to capacity with everyone adorned in white with a touch of blue. Blue was Nana's favorite color. The choir sounded angelic, the Holy Ghost fell, and a praise broke out. I don't remember if I danced or not, but it was at that moment I knew that this is the kind of church Nana would have loved. It's from that point on that I no longer looked at the service as a funeral. This was my first experience of a Homegoing service.

The next day was the burial, which was the most painful thing I ever had to witness because, until this point, I have never seen my Pops cry outside of praising God. The sound that came from him as they put Nana in the ground shook me to the core and shattered every piece of my heart. To this day, I do not know what happened to me. I do not know if I passed out or not, but the next thing I recall is being in the limousine with my cousins.

I do not think any of us spoke a word the whole ride back to the church. Beyond that point, the rest of the year is blank. I don't remember what I did or how I made it through school. I just remember frequent trips to Trenton, NJ, and then it was summertime.

CHAPTER 5

As the summer of 1993 approached, I came home from school, and my Pop sat me down and explained to me he had an opportunity to make a lot of money for us, but he had to go away for three months to get it. He also told me if I wasn't going to be comfortable with him being gone that long, he would stay and figure something else out. He told me that he would be in Germany for three months starting in November, and my uncle and my aunt would be there to check on me. My godbrother would move in to make sure I was up for school and to look out for me. Pop didn't realize I was cool with it when he first told me, but I was. This was the first time since Nana passed that I saw excitement in him.

Then I got extra excited when he told me that I would fly out to Germany for Christmas if I kept my grades up while he was gone. By this time, I was so engulfed in church and started hanging out with people from other churches. I started following and singing in the choir with my other godbrother,

Jeffrey Young. School had become easy because I just wanted to do what I had to do to get to the weekend and go to different church services and then out to eat.

The time went so fast everything was a blur. Before I knew it, it was time to go to Germany for Christmas. As I prepared to go, I had a list of things I was going to do once I was there. I went to the airport and met with my godsister, who is younger than me. We were so excited to go overseas. The flight was so long that I started to feel like we were never going to get there. Finally, after hours of flying, we landed, and all I could think was, *wow, we are really here.*

My pops met us at the airport. He began talking about how I was doing in school and what classes I needed to focus on. I was amazed. How did he know what I've been doing at home? I was not bothered by it at all. I just wanted to go all over the place in Germany and talk about the school stuff later.

The first night we were there, my pops had to sing in a show. That was the reason he came to Germany. He is an amazing singer. I felt like a star. I saw people clapping and singing, and they did not know any English. They took pictures with him. It was all amazing to witness. People came to take us to eat, to talk to us, and to ask us how we felt about being there. They wanted to know if we were enjoying ourselves in Germany. It was a great experience for me. During the flight home, it finally hit me that I really had a father. I had a family waiting for me at the airport when I returned. And more importantly, I had a support system that made sure I had everything I needed and even some of what I wanted.

CHAPTER 6

The year was 1994, and my high school graduation was coming soon. I had some challenges in math, but I was determined to walk across that stage. I went to a tutor after school to make sure I met my goal. Everything seemed to be working for me.

I had a steady schedule, a loving family, and my own room. Everything was great until one Sunday, while I was at church, I saw my biological cousin. She told me that she saw my mom and gave me her address. I can remember it like it was yesterday.

"You know I'm your family," she said. "You need to go see your mother. She's been asking for you."

I was so confused. Confused because part of me was happy to hear my mother was looking for me, but then the other part of me was mad because I felt like my biological cousin saw that I was happy and felt like she had to rob me of my happiness. Either way, I mentioned to Pops what had happened. He was quiet for a while, and then he asked me what I wanted to do. I hesitated for a minute because I really did not know what to do. But before I knew it, my mouth said I wanted to see her. Everything beyond that is blank. Next thing I know, me and my pops were sitting in my mother's two-bedroom apartment with Charlene. My mom had just had a baby boy.

Here I was again with all kinds of crazy emotions that I still can't describe. *Another baby? Wow. Did she forget about me when she had this boy? Did she hate me? Did she ever love me? Why now when everything is finally coming together? Why would she send word for me to come see her?*

Even with all the crazy thoughts running through my head, I was still happy to see her. I just started telling her all the great things that were happening for me and all the places I was going and all the things I was learning.

She just smiled and said, "That's good. I knew Alvin would take care of you."

Then I said it. Before I could even think, I said it to her because I was so caught up with all the accomplishments I made. I never thought about how she felt, but it was obvious she was still suffering from her substance abuse. It had started to take a toll on her appearance, but I didn't care because, in my mind, she still looked the same, and I said it without considering how she felt.

"I'm graduating from high school, and you can come to my graduation."

She smiled and said, "We'll see because I really don't have anything to wear.

I guess Pop saw the look on my face because he immediately replied to her.

"Don't worry. We will come pick you up before time and buy you whatever you need to make it."

"Okay, I will be there."

I was so excited. Words could never express the joy I had when my mom said she would come to my graduation. I was on a natural high for the rest of the week. Every day I thought about what my graduation day would be like—the pictures, the laughter, and going out to eat afterward. I had the whole day planned out in my head.

The following week, they gave us our graduation tickets to give to our family. Needless to say, I couldn't wait to get home so Pop and I could get my mom and buy her something and give her the ticket.

Things were so great. The sun was out, I was graduating from high school, and I found my mom. I got home and gave Pop the tickets. We called my mother and told her we were on our way to pick her up to buy her something to wear. We got to her house, and Pop blew the horn. She didn't come outside. He blew the horn again. Still nothing. No response.

"Maybe she can't hear the horn," I said.

I got out and rang her doorbell. No response. Nothing. Just nothing.

I rang it again. This time I backed up so she could see me from her window. I saw her peek out the side of the blinds and go away from the window. My body said she was coming to open the door, but my mind already knew that she wasn't coming down. I stood there for about a minute, and finally Pop said,

"Come on, Ro. Let's go. She's not coming."

I walked back to the car, crushed to my soul.

Pop said, "Don't worry. I'll be there, and we are going to have a great time."

"Okay," I said, but on the inside, I was broken. All the old feelings I thought were over suddenly resurfaced. I felt like that little boy who was left in the shelter alone.

We went home and ate Chinese food. My Pop played Nintendo with me all night. It was then that I realized that I was no longer that kid left at the shelter. I was now a young man with a father who loved him enough to make sure I knew that I mattered without saying a word. A couple of days before my graduation, Pop asked me what I wanted for graduation. Without hesitation, I told him I wanted to change my name to the only family I knew.

"Are you sure?" he asked.

"Absolutely, Pops."

On my graduation day, as I walked across the stage, I shut the door to Leonard Romarr Washington and all the bad memories with it. I walked into manhood and my new season as D'maine Romarr Freeland.

These are the Confessions of a Church Boy. On this journey, I've learned that legacy is not carried by blood but by those who exhibit all the morals and standards handed down to them.

www.ingramcontent.com/pod-product-compliance
Lightning Source LLC
Chambersburg PA
CBHW051713090426
42736CB00013B/2689